~ALL THAT IS WORTH TELLING~

Poetic IN sights along the path

(with INteractive elements for the reader)

by

Katherine Kaufman

Copyright © 2025 by Katherine Kaufman

All rights reserved. No part of this book may be used or reproduced or transmitted in any form, in any manner, by any means whatsoever, including electronic or mechanical, including photocopying, recording, or from any information storage retrieval system, without written permission from the author except in the case of brief quotations embodied in reviews or academic studies.

Cover images and images contained in this book are all Public Domain or Free to Use or are original images created by the author.
Cover Design: Christine K. Niver

ISBN: 979-8-218-62077-6

For information email:
KatherineKbooks@proton.me

This book is dedicated to my mother,
Frances—
who always supported and encouraged my creativity,
even when she didn't always understand or agree with my expressions.

She gave me something rare and sacred:
the freedom to be myself.

A lifelong lover of books,
this one is for her.

Thank you, Mom.
You are forever alive in my heart.

Contents

Introduction 6
The Things I Write 9
Group 1 What I Need
to Know Today 10
  -Eternal Thanks 11
  -Fear is not the Enemy ... 12
  -Final Crossing 13
  -I Belong to That 14
  -Lead with Your Heart 15
  -My Heart Knows Better 16
  -No Fear in here 17
  -Final Battle 18
  -True Gold 19
-Shiva's Game   20
  -Transformation 22

Group 2 -Nature 23
  -Gentle Rain 24
  -I Found My Garden 25
  -In This Shining Morning 26
  -Love Rising 27
  -Restless Roots 28
  -September Battle 29
  -The Everlasting Cycle ...30
  -The 1st Green Sprout 31
  -The Glory of Day & Night 32
  -The Shooting Star 33
  -When the Spices are Right 34

Group 3 -Relationships ...35
  -A Dance With Love 36
   Across The Bay 37
  -Aura Pleasure 38
  -Baba's Eyes 39
  -Do You Remember 40
  -Dreaming & Waking Up
     Together 41
  -Encore 42
  -Ever 43
  -I Know You 44
  -One Fallen Angel 45
  -Paper Cut 46
  -Permanently Blind 47
  -Put on Your Glasses 48
  -Removing the Mask 49
  -Remembering How To Fly
     50
  -Song Of Oneness 52
  -Surrender 53
  -The Beginning 54
  -The Sweet 55
  -The Quiet Man 56
  -To Be Always Free 57
  -True Love 58
  -Welcome 59
  -When My Sister Laughs 60
Group 4- From the darker
     side 61

- Dharma 62
- God Has Shown 63
- I Crawled Down Into the
    Center of my Heart 64
- I Remember Yesterday 65
- Just Breathe 66
- New Life 67
- Thursday 68
- To Be Free From Fear 69
- What Are You Looking At 70

Group 5- Is this real 71
- Artoficial Untelligence 72
- Indigestion 73
- no reply 74
- The Dream 75
- The Juice 76
- Time Flies 77
- What It Is 78

Group 6- Shifting
    Frequencies 79
- Because You Said Yes 80
- Born Day 81
- Break The Cycle 82
- Feel The Umph 83
- No Small Dreams 84
- Notes To Self 85
- One Liners 86
- Self Inspired 87
- Lessons of Patience 88
- The Time of Your Life 89

- To Do List 90
- Too Old 91
- Sing Sing Sing 92

Group 7-
    Higher Realms 93
- Break Dancing 94
- I Am Silent 95
- Message 96
- Prayer 97
- Praying Hands 98
- The Edges of Life 99
- The True Value of
    Memory 100
- What Is Peace 101
- What Price 102
- All That Is Worth
    Telling 103

About The Author 104

*IN*TRODUCTION

Life has many ups and downs, twists and turns, ins and outs, wonderful surprises and tragic downfalls, inspiring challenges and quiet moments of inner reflection. Yet, through it all, there is one common thread: your self. You are the one who experiences it all.

~ These poems were mostly written at a time in my life when great upheavals and extremes of life, both highs and lows, were happening. A voice began speaking distinctly inside me that essentially dictated these poems to me at unpredictable, yet perfect, moments.

~ For years, the poems sat unread as I went on with the changes in my life. Now, I have been called to collect them together and read them again. The most amazing thing is that they mean more to me today than they did when I wrote them almost 30 years ago. I realize that what is happening on the planet and in my life right now is the reason these poems were written. Each one has a distinct wisdom and message that is both timely and timeless.

~ There is a voice within that speaks guidance and truth to each of us, that comes from what some call Source, Creator, God, The Universe, the Eternal Inner Self, and many other names. This is the voice that has spoken to me through all these poems.

It speaks to your inner self, too. These poems may even spark a conversation between you and your own Source—the Source of Love that has created us all and connects us to everything.

~ Each of the poems has its own feeling, for which I have chosen specific visual keys—a certain font, a layout that creates a rhythm and pattern, some with background images or small pictures. These details have been added to this current collection but have all been inspired by the same Source, the inner voice that dictated the poems originally.

~ If you like, start with a question or ask for inspiration. Then, open to a random page and see what message you get there. Or choose from one of the group headings that are just general themes that I discovered as I was organizing the collection. Or simply choose a title that reaches out to you.

~ Above all, play and enjoy the experience and surprises that come into your awareness. Make your own notes or drawings in the margins. Make each poem yours in your own way. Once you've read them, they become a part of you to explore and expand on. Maybe write your own book of all that is worth telling, whatever that may be. You can make use of the blank pages at the back of the book, for your own thoughts, words, or art.

~What, to you, is worth telling?
What are you IN spired to tell?~

α THE THINGS I WRITE ω

Could the things I write become the truth
of my life?
An epic journey of D'Light?
A grand escapade?
An ode to magnificence!
A legendary romance!
An invitation to the dance?
A timeless tale of terrific proportions
(With some minor distortions).
So very absurd!
Yet, all in a word
That, somehow, leads me Home?!

~Group 1~

What I need to know today

ETERNAL THANKS

The thanks we give *fills* in all the gaps
Between *yesterdayandtomorrow*
And centers us right where we are ~
Today.
When we recognize all the gifts that are
present in the present,
We shine the light on that which is pleasing to
us.
Light gives life.
This is how we continue to have Joy in our lives
~ By continuing to see it as happening in
this moment
And to acknowledge it.

The vibration of thanks giving reverberates
With wisdom and grace.
It allows us to know and effortlessly express
Our true nature in this eternal now
As we constantly renew what is in our
hearts.
Let us give thanks. Let us be who we are.

FEAR IS NOT THE ENEMY

Fear is not the enemy.
It's just a little child
Trying to remember how to smile.

Faith is not our savior.
It's just a way of looking at the world
And seeing a friend.

Hate is not a reason to kill or be killed.
It's just an innocent cry
For a love reply.

VI

Final Crossing

What are these tears I have for you,
    my old friend and foe,
My old lover and nemesis?
Can we rise up together or must one of us fall?
It is not an unnatural fear, but a natural
    mourning
As I say good bye to all we ever had in this old world
That we've given our lives and breadths to.
That world grows dim, now.

But, beyond the veil of tears shines a new Sun,
Brighter than before.
That is where I want to go.
So I must close this book and leave it behind Forever
To begin a new story that has yet to be written
In all Creation.

This time, the possibilities are Truly endless.

I BELONG TO THAT

It is not this life for me
To do with,
But, to be pleased.
Nor is it this wealth to make or spend.
Nor this debt to pay or not.
Nor this job to do or quit.
Nor this body to wake or sleep or feed or clothe.
These are all just incidentals, extenuating
      circumstances to enjoy along this way.

I am That breath that circulates,
That sound it makes,
That silence between takes.
That hollow space in back of the eyes
Is where an expanding universe lies.
A reality there grows and glows
Brighter than the blinding spotlights of this life.
Enlightenment is a focus on That.
That is my Self
My Self IS That.

      I belong to That.

♥LEAD WITH YOUR HEART

Your heart keeps the rhythm
That your soul can dance to.
It is an instinctive beat
That, if you let it, it will move your feet
To a certain step in a certain direction
That will lead you to where you want to Be.
It's that steady vibration that keeps you alive.
Sleeping or waking or dreaming you thrive.
Your center of yearning.
Your core of discerning.
Your light of Love always burning.
A constant reminder from your Source
That you are a part of an eternal, ongoing movement
That is cosmically choreographed.
You can find your steps if you simply listen
And feel the beat.

MY HEART KNOWS BETTER

My heart beats at a rate
That paces my life.
I may go rushing around
Trying to
Get things done or
Fix them or
Feel better or
See them sprout.
But, they don't happen
Until my heart has beaten
A certain number of beats.
No matter how hard I try and push and run and jump and keep at it,
My heartbeat rules the road.
I know, because,
When I tune into it,
I feel its momentum and rate and
I follow it
And everything, in its own time,
Comes to its proper fruition
And smiles at me.
But, when I forget to listen,
I only frustrate myself and cause myself pain.
This is what heartache is:
Me, fighting against the natural movement of things.
My heart knows better.

NO FEAR in here

There is no Holiday out here.
No stars shining brightly.
No cheer.

All of our money is gone.
No presents to open.
No song.

Friends have forgotten us.
Children aren't laughing.
No trust.

Our hands and feet are cold.
We're coughing and shivering.
No gold.

There is no Holiday out here.
It's time to come inside,
My dear.
It's time to come inside.
No fear

The Final Battle

*In the midst of Battle,
I chose not to fight.
The angels came round me
And blinded me with Light.*

*Suddenly, with Thunder,
As words of Truth, I spoke,
The darkness fell asunder
In terror, as it broke.*

*It crawled away in shame and guilt
Never to return.
And all the falseness it had built
Crumbled down and burned.*

*The Storm now clears away all fears.
The Sun returns to Shine.
The moon releases Joyful tears
That heal the poisoned mind.*

*Now, Rise up, Glorious Being!
The angels say to me.
Let Love Be what you're feeling
And You are finally free.*

TRUE GOLD

There is a world,
A golden world
That shimmers
Just behind the cold, gray sky,
Just beneath the layers of dust,
Just inside the coatings of crust
Around the weary heart.

The veil of tears,
Created by doubts and fears,
Is just purification,
The process of transformation
By which perception becomes completely clear.
Rain falls.
Clouds break.
Dust scatters.
Crust shatters.
What matters
Is seen as a golden glow.
And the true surprise? To realize
That the source of this light
Is one's own unwavering devotion.

SHIVA'S* GAME

This is Shiva's game.
Mist climbing the mountainsides,
Curling up in the gray sky.
Colliding air masses.
Thundering bolts of enlightenment.
Torrential walls of wash.
The sweetest of summer sighs.
This is Shiva's game.
Take it to the edge of time
And bring it back.
Turn it upside down
And twist it inside out.
Open up a cocoon of worms.
Give them wings to fly.
This is Shiva's game.
Eyes are closed eyes are open.
Hands are closed hands are open.
Feet are still feet are dancing.

Mind is still heart is dancing.
Consciousness plays
Everywhere here and there.
This is Shiva's game.
We have all been invited to play.
We have all said "Yes".
Some will want to win.
Some will want to lose.
Some will deny it is a game
Or that it exists at all
But, they have forgotten who they really ARE and want to BE
Re~minded.
This is Shiva's game.

---

*In Indian tradition and philosophy, Shiva is the embodiment of the aspect of God that gives rise to the essence and movement of all things, also known as "the play of divine consciousness".

TRANSFORMATION

*The process that goes on to unfold
the layers of life
Is like turning the pages of a book
that is ever more fascinating.
And when you reach the final page,
You turn to the beginning again and
read it as if for the first time.
Only, the understanding is much
deeper
So that it seems to be a whole new
book.
But, it is you who are new,
Transformed by the process itself, in
each moment.*

~Group 2~

Nature

GENTLE RAIN

Gentle rain
    Falls
        Tells
A story of those gentle tears
That give rise
        To blessed life.
Each drop,
    A letting go of fears,
        Trickling down
            Into thirsty roots.
Soon,
    Green is seen
        Blossoming
In a place
    Where before, there was
only a yearning
        To **grow**

I FOUND MY GARDEN

I found my garden
When I looked within.
Every flower, every tree,
Every fragrant blossom
I'd ever dreamed of, peacefully,
All growing in
My real garden inside.
My bed of pure light,
My source of true delight
Where showers and colors swirl with sound
And graceful breezes abound.
When I select the fruit, gently,
It nourishes, completely.
It feeds itself, sweetly,
And grows, again,
Even more deeply.
I bow to its beauty
And let the release of my joyful tears
Be humble drops of kind moisture.
A transforming energy,
Rich with fertility
That gives as it receives
An elegant harmony
In a cycle of pure wonder.
I found my perfect garden
Growing within.

~In This Shining Morning

In this shining morning
The Light of Heart is reflected in the sky.

In this shining morning
All leaves sparkle like
        so many emerald clusters.

In this shining morning
Imperfections of my vision are purified.

In this shining morning
    I place my faith

LOVE RISING

As we walk upon this generous earth,
We give it our gifts and it turns into heaven.
We share our breath with the multitudes of trees and plants.
We let our messages be carried on the songs of the wind.
We bow to the eternal mountains
And float upon the cleansing waters.
We extend our grateful arms and embrace the sheltering sky.
We vibrate thunder with the claps of our hands
As we applaud the flashing lightnings of startling beauty.
We laugh with the full moon in our hearts
And as we kiss the fragrant dawn in our minds,
We can see the colors of Love coming over the horizon.

RESTLESS ROOTS

I am underground
Where roots seek nourishment
And something to hold onto
To stay in one place,
So to grow deeper.
Roots are at the base of stems, trunks and leaves
That take in the Sun from above
So to grow higher~
How to use the food
Cannot be separated.
My roots must have stems.
My roots must be a foundation for
What reaches up.
Both light and dark
Feed me.

SEPTEMBER BATTLE

Oak trees are hurling down their
seeds to the ground.
They smack the earth with the force
of a determined bullet.
I am an innocent bystander
Living in the midst of a battle for
survival.
My house is constantly pelted with
acorn grenades.
I find tiny unexploded acorn bombs
on my deck.
I fear for my windows.
But, I understand that the will to live
Can sometimes seem violent.

In nature's scheme of things,
the casualties
Must be worth it.

THE EVERLASTING CYCLE

I take walks around the woods, here.
The trees seem to stand tall for me.

They bow and wave as breezes blow.
In autumn, they put on sunset colors
Then, let them fall, scattering like confetti
As if in celebration,
Leaving the ground newly splotched in dappled light.

Against a perfect blue sky that never ends,
They tell their stories like ancient teachers who know the meaning of life.

They've seen so many cycles,

They understand birth and death as part of the same oneness.

As I walk, they tell me to lift up my heart and mind.

There is no season for sadness.

Even in the time of dying, they create their beauty that is immeasurable.

They know it is not an ending, but, part of an ongoing cycle that has the wisdom to continue,

Though we may forget that we are in it.

THE FIRST GREEN SPROUT

I spotted the first green sprout of spring.
It caught my eye
Like an emerald, glinting,
In the mist of sleeping gray stone.
I stopped to admire its perfection.
It glanced back at me and I saw
Myself sprouting, there.
I recognized the ancient yearly ritual
When the human spirit looks out of a
quiet winter shelter and sees
Nature extending its delicately inviting
tendrils
As a sweet reminder that it's time, again,
To laugh and shine and grow.
There is no guesswork.
It is all designed, already,
Perfectly.
We just follow the cues.

THE GLORY OF DAY AND NIGHT

It is day, vibrantly.
It is night, quietly.
One breath and
I wrap my arms around it all.

Inside the heart's deep hollow canyon,
I listen to the sound.
It echoes through inner space,
Creating movement in a shimmering pattern,
like a patchwork blanket,
A quilt of fine resonance
In my soul.
Constantly, it shakes with exuberant volume.
If I stand in this,
I feel the wave of energy running up through my
heels to my head,
Rushing into the sky,
Circling out and around and back and down.
This is the sound that gives me life.

As I spin, gracefully, across the canyon,
I weave myself into the patchwork pattern
And sing the glory of day and night.

THE SHOOTING STAR

I remember a moonlit night
When a shooting star fell out of the sky
And into my heart.
It caused a great tidal wave in the ocean of my soul.
It burned up my complacent home,
All the while, illuminating my destiny.
Now, I long to walk the path
That leads out of darkness
And which beckons like a perfect lover.

Since that night, I am transformed by my steps.
Wind whips at my whims.
Rain races through my veins.
Though I have wandered off, at times,
I realize I only beat a new path,
Another way, for those who may follow.
Sometimes I feel lost.
But, then, I can feel the star, pulsing,
And I follow That.

WHEN THE SPICES ARE RIGHT

When the spices are right
Then spirit can flow
From the nose to the tongue
To the throat to the glow
That is felt deep inside.
It begins in the heart,
Warms the center,
Moves out to each part
Till all Being vibrates
With the glory of Love
From root below
To crown above.
Now, hard thoughts can soften.
Hurt thoughts can heal,
Whole and contented,
Grateful for the meal.
Prepared by such hands
That are guided by God's measure,
When the spices are right
We can taste God's pleasure.

~Group 3~

Relationships

A DANCE WITH LOVE

And Lord Ganesh* said to me, "Thank you for
Remembering me...
Always your protector
Always here.
You carry me in your heart.
When you lose your balance, I catch you
And we swirl together and dance.
But you never fall
It becomes instead, a joyous experience of fun
and you never fall.
I won't let you fall
Ever.
Let it all be a dance with Love
and you'll never fall.
That is your protection and
The rest is
Already Done.
This is my gift to you because you remembered
me.
AUM."
*Oh Ganesh, Thank you
For reminding me to remember you.
AUM*

*In Indian philosophy and tradition, Lord Ganesh represents the embodiment of the aspect of God that is protection and the remover of obstacles.

ACROSS THE BAY

Come on,
San Francisco!
Are you going?
Where's your heart?
Slipping into the ocean.
Waves of emotion
Pull you apart.

A golden mind
Makes a bridge
To a golden life.
Sweet breath of morning mist
Quietly lifts
And makes rainbows as you look
Across the bay.
Like a good sun,
You know how to shine on
And on.

Come
Down.
Smell the roses, today.
Make your way
Home.

AURA PLEASURE

It's what you don't say that says the most.
The thing that lingers is not the words you've spoken.
It's not the phrase you utter that makes time stop for a moment.
When you speak your mind, it's not the sentences that I understand.
The verbal expressions are not what make sense.
This language is not grammatically correct.
I don't know what you've said,
But, I know exactly what you mean.
So...
Tell me more.

BABA'S EYES

In your eyes, I see the fertile earth that nourishes life.
I see the perfect jewels that reflect transcendent light.
In your eyes, I see depth of heart, devotional fire,
The compassion of one who knows no desire.
In your eyes, I see all the way back to the beginning of time and into eternity, now.
I see all the answers to all the questions that have ever been asked and will ever be.
How?

In your eyes, I see the smile of a child,
The stars and the heavens,
Cascading waterfalls and still
Mirror-like pools which reflect the one who is looking.
(I dive into the Ocean of Brilliance.)

In your eyes, I see my own gaze transfixed
Upon my own Self.
I see So'ham (I am That).

How blessed to be seen by the Guru*.
How divine to live in that moment!

*A True Guru can only reflect back to you that which is your True Self

DO YOU REMEMBER?

Do you remember when we were one?
It was when we first met –
When we were so small and everything was growing so tall.
When we were young and everything was young at heart.
When every new color made us embrace the rainbow.
We asked no questions. We only played.
We clapped our hands and we were brave.
When we ran away, we always ended up at home.
When we hurt ourselves, we'd laugh together and heal the wounds.
We sang a song and forgot the pain.
We tasted goodness and felt good, again.
We treasured yesterday and dreamed of tomorrow.
We felt so special to be so much the same.
We looked up at the sky and it told us we could fly.
We could jump into the murky water and still see all the way to the bottom.
Fire could not burn us. It would only light our way.
Earth could not bury us. It would only offer us everlasting peace.
Friends would greet us and invite us in.
On a lonesome road, we knew that we were not alone.
We walked together. We shared a home.
We could see the blending of our hearts, so warm
And blessed with gifts
Like rays of light from an eternal Sun.
Do remember when we were One?
Not so long ago...
It was just...
Today.

DREAMING AND WAKING UP TOGETHER

Saying goodbye.
Letting the past go.
Letting you go on your way.
Maybe I don't have to remember you anymore.
Maybe this is the end of the dream.
I will awaken into the bright, sunny day
That is all Light and Love.
And yes,
You'll be there, too.
The one who never smiles
Will be beaming, grinning ear to ear
And laughter will be heard ringing
'Round the universe... Come on...
Meet you on the other side.
Let's Be Free.
This is what I mean by
"I Love You."

ENCORE

Enter into the house of joy.
Reach out and embrace the crowd.
They await your entrance to the stage.
In your sunny heart lies truth.
In your peaceful mind lies grace.
As you enter, majestically,
The crowd rises and applauds.
You have come to give your greatest performance.
But, it is no "act" for you.
It is the simple gift of your Love of life
That you share, freely, with everyone.
There is no greater part that could be played.
So, you deserve to take a bow...
The crowd wants an encore!
You never let them down.

EVER

I thought I was lonely.
But, that was when I forgot you are here.
I forgot you go everywhere with me,
Walk by my side,
Fill in all the spaces
Between my breaths.

I want to see you everywhere.
But, I carry you with me
So, you are there.
You are there...
You are there...

You are HERE
Deep Love
Of my life.

Let me not forget you,
Ever.

I KNOW YOU

You are in the center of my heart.

That is where I'd like you to stay.

I'm not sure how you got there.

Perhaps, you were there from the start,

Only, I just discovered you.

Now, I'd like to know you better and better

Until I don't miss you anymore.

Until I know You

as my Self.

~ONE FALLEN ANGEL~

One fallen angel, one broken wing.
Another fallen angel, another broken wing.
Each one wounded, shot down from the sky.
Picking up the pieces. Letting out a sigh.
Looking up to heaven to the distant light,
One angel hides away, the other learns to fight.
Waiting for the moment, so patient and so sure.
Still happy to be here with heart so pure.
Day after day, each wanders the planet
Sowing seeds of kindness into souls of solid granite.
Meeting up with strangers, hoping to share a smile.
Each keeping their head up for a little while.
Then, one fine day, while forgetting the broken wing,
They bumped into each other and started to sing.
Each gently took the other's heart into hand.
Now they could remember. Now they could understand
The power of their joy can heal every heart here.
A sweet inspiration to let go of fear.
Two fallen angels look up to the sky.
Each offers one wing to the other.
Now together, they can fly.

PAPER CUT

Cold blue words on stark icy white pages.
Opaque razor-thin turns slice through fingers
With a merciless edge, drawing spiritual blood
Like no steel sword ever could.
I wince and what is written falls to the floor.
For days on end, then, I stagger around with a gaping wound,
Crying out to be fixed up by a faith healer.

He approaches, clutching a familiar, though dog-eared, manual.
I recognize the book he treasures.
I can tell each blood stained page used to be
A cold stark icy white.
But, the blood is now long since dried and the words there
Are smooth-edged and warm.

He turns yet another page
And takes my hand.
I look inside the kindness of his eyes and find my pain
Fading, soothed away, becoming grateful.

After so many days, now, and many more nights of wandering,
Still, the wound weeps once in awhile. I can't remember why
The memory, hazy.
I want to pick up the book again. I turn the page.
The words don't seem so cold, now.
The cut is not so cruel and somehow,
Instead of pain, there is kindness
And the holding of a hand.

PERMANENTLY BLIND

Zip your coat up, now.
Keep yourself warm as you step outside.
You might feel the wind hit you
Too close to the bone
And you'll shiver through and through.
You might believe that the world
Is always so cold and harsh
And you'll retreat, again and lose your
chance, again.
But, wait and see the wind calms down
around you.
The clouds move away,
The sun shines on you, sweetly, and
Makes you feel welcome
Like you belong here
In the wide world
That is as kind as your hands are open.
You can reach out
Even if you have to wear gloves
To keep your fingers from freezing.
You belong here
Under the bright blue sky
That is as honest as your eyes are open.
You can look around
Even if you have to wear shades
To keep from going
permanently blind.

PUT ON YOUR GLASSES

I look for the order. You lead me through the chaos of order
    And show me the order in chaos.
I look for the movement. You move me
    To stillness.
I look for the flow of thought.
    You just flow.
I look for you in my dreams. You come in
    And wake me up.
I would give you a token for passage across the bridge of knowledge.
You've already been over and back again
    And never even noticed you had to pay.
I look to remember the meaning. You let me
Put on your glasses and I forget what I've been looking for
    And just See

REMOVING THE MASK

Each of us wears a mask of fear
And it is the task of another of us to, gently,
remove it.
Fear is what, we believe, protects us.
But, it only prevents our True Being from showing
through.
It is a hard outer shell that we must look past
To the beauty within.
When you see someone wearing the mask of fear,
The way to eliminate it is to
1st, realize it is an innocent mistake.
2nd, to know it is not necessary.
3rd, to use inner vision to transcend the illusion of
it.
At this point, it will become loose and transparent.
Light will begin to show through and
Hardness will give way to laughter.
The mask will crumble and fall away.
The face of your beloved will shine upon you.
At that moment, you will realize that you, yourself,
No longer wear a mask.
You have forgotten what fear means
And you are free.
You will remember
Nothing but Love.
You will see
Nothing but Love

REMEMBERING HOW TO FLY

I hear someone say "hello".
It wakes me up from a dream.
Where am I?
A hand takes mine and lifts me to my feet
And then, in a little while, up off my feet
into the sky.
How did I get here?

The hand still holds mine.
I cannot even ask whose it is.
I am in awe and I am trying to take it all in.
Look down there.
Everyone down there is dreaming to fly.
Oh, could I, would I even swoop down and
grab a hand
To let them know they can?
And so, in that moment, I am reaching for a
hand and taking it.
I pull this one up and up.
How could I even do this without the one who
took mine?

And in turning my head around for the first time,
I see that the other hand of the one who took mine
Is being held up by another and that one to another and on and on So far, I cannot see the end of it.
Already, the one whose hand I took has reached down
To lift up one more.
Somehow, at that moment, I feel lighter.

So, this is how to fly!
Yes, I remember hearing this story in a dream:
We can all fly, but only if we fly together.
And so the next one reaches to lift up the next one
That lifts us all
Even higher.

So, it is not a dream, after all!

SONG OF ONENESS

The sun is long.
The wind is short.
My breath is yours under the moon.
Tied like vines wrapped surely together,
We swing and sway.
We play like doves.
There's no tomorrow.
Only the Song of Oneness
That tells of a world in love with peace
And joining of hearts and spirits
That fly into stars to give them light.
As we breath, they flicker and grow bright.
As we dance, they burn with delight.
As we sleep, they watch and keep Love in sight.
What we have found is true, tonight.
What we have found is true.

SURRENDER(the Beloved)

With your lips
You part my lips.
Your tongue is so long.
It touches my soul.
It enters my heart.
Every cell and fiber of my being
Submits to your enchanting rhythm.
I lose myself and become you.
I surrender to your perfect
command.
You command me to surrender.
You are the masterful One.
I let you take me and take me
Until I am gone,
Indistinguishable from Love, ItSelf.

THE BEGINNING

We sleep together.
Our dream is one.

We wake together.
Our dream is done.

We live together.
Our hope lives on.

We Love together.
Our life's begun.

THE SWEET

How did you know
I needed to dance?
A kick in the pants?
Up on my feet
Without a thought.
I'm movin', I'm groovin'.
My spirits are lifting
High.

How did you know
I wanted to laugh?
Double over in half?
Spill out all the dark
Inside my mind.
What did I find?
Nothing but melodies
And harmonies and a beat...
So sweet
Soooo much
Sweeeeeter than sweet.
 ...Tasty... how did you know?

THE QUIET MAN

The quiet man does not speak of
his inner silence.
Yet, it permeates the moment in his
presence.
The silence is so loud, it drowns out
the din, the chatter.
The silence takes all the things that
seem alone and merges them.
The result is a silent connection
That excludes not a thing.
The result is Love.
The quiet man makes you feel
welcome
Without a word.
When you reach to touch him,
You only find your own Self,
Which is all you can ever know
And all there IS to know.
And so,
You become as silent as
the quiet man.

TO BE ALWAYS FREE

Never dying. Always growing.
Never wishing. Always knowing.
Always richer. Never poor.
Never doubting. Always sure.

Light and comfort. Silent sound.
Never empty. Never bound.
Ageless, timeless, spaceless Mind.
Vision true. Thought aligned.

Ever present. Never far.
Ever shining, constant star.
Never doing. Always done.
Never wanting. Always One.

May you choose to Be
Always Free

TRUE LOVE

My Love for you reaches far beyond this world.
Its roots extend to...
Beyond the describable,
Beyond the thinkable.
It sustains me like breath
And blood.
But, it is also what makes my heart beat.

My Love for you fills me to bursting,
Unshackles my being,
Defies my boundaries,
Breaks my will,
Restores my faith.
It makes me forget who I thought I was
And lets me become who I Am.

My Love for you touches my soul with beauty
So painfully exquisite, I must cry.
It overtakes me.
I must bow down to it and surrender.
It is too much for me, alone, to bear.
So, I must share my Love for you
With All.

~ WELCOME ~

Come closer.
Come as close as you like.
I will not ask you to leave.
It's like this:
The closer you come to me,
The more serene I become.

See into my eyes.
Step into my shoes.
Hold my hand.
Let your breath fall upon my cheek
And into my ear.
It is mine, now.
I won't give it back.
I will not ask you to leave.

Welcome
Come as close as you can.
Come closer.
Closer.
Come
And Be

Welcome

WHEN MY SISTER LAUGHS

There's a certain laughter
That can move the earth.
It vibrates deeply in the soul
Then magnifies and expands
exponentially
Until it bursts forth like a quake
From the throat and mouth and across
the face
Of the one who witnesses the cosmic joke
And gets it.

The body rocks.
The ripples radiate out and give
A relaxing massage to the troubles of
the universe.

Even the echoing tremors,
The memories of those laughs,
Can make you smile,
again.

~Group 4~

From the darker side

DHARMA

Though shadows may unite
      behind the open doors
And beneath the waves
      Terror may
   Tear away at eternal faith,
Eternal faith still
    Stands like a sentry guarding
       The Way
With infinite layers to penetrate
 Visible through empty eyes
      Led by Voices of Light
Heard through golden ears
   Old and older than peace.

We will sail.
We will dance.
We will sink.
We will die never
And ever we will live
As we believe
In our souls.
   I remember traveling ahead
And never looking back.
   Learning to sing
From my true heart,
Finding my light and my faith
   beneath the waves and
        Even behind the doors.

GOD HAS SHOWN

Today, God has shown me pain, not to punish me.
But, to show me that pain does not overshadow love.

Today, God has shown me despair, not to forsake me.
But, to show me that a light still shines way down there.

Today, God has shown me death, not to be unfair.
But, to let me see that the Spirit lives on.

Today, God has shown me loneliness, not to be cruel.
But, to make me look inward and find my connection with Everything.

Today, God has shown me destitution, not to make me sacrifice.
But, to teach me to give everything, in order to have everything.

Today, God has shown me humanity, not to point out flaws.
But, to give me a reason to share the wisdom of what He has shown me
And let that light become brighter for all.

I CRAWLED DOWN INTO THE CENTER OF MY HEART

I crawled down into the center of my heart
And found the truth.
I did not have to beg, borrow or steal.
I only had to ask and it was revealed.
I imagined walking through fire and flood to get to it.
I conjured up false images of pain and betrayal to make myself feel worthy to receive it.
But, in the end,
I bowed down so deeply and humbly to my inner grace
That I found the way to a quiet request~~~

And there it was...the Truth.
And there I Am.

I Remember Yesterday

Yesterday

I only wanted to live

And only wanted to give

        Today

        I only wanted to die

        And only wondered

        Why?

                Tomorrow

            I only feel and see

            What is next for me...

Becomes another memory

        And then

                Another memory

And then   Another memory

JUST BREATHE

*A deep choking sadness drapes over me
From nowhere.
        A scary feeling to feel that sad and not
                  know why.
It's so unbearable.
I feel like I'd do anything to stop it…maybe
Even k*ll myself.   as if death exists
But I know that won't end it.
That 'll only continue the pattern so I don't do it.*

*Instead,
I pray that the Light inside of me will show itself
And heal me.
I pray until I feel better and I do feel better,
Eventually in Time. time. time.
I pray until I feel the sad drape over me has
been lifted.
I can breathe and feel the Sun again.*

*Then,
I take rest;
Lay down in a peaceful safe place and sleep, if
sleep comes.
Or
Just breathe for awhile…just…breathe*

NEW LIFE

My own unlimited pain.
The sobbing feels fine like a grateful liberation.
All I thought I ever had is now gone.
I now know I have everything
Because I need nothing.

It is difficult to look at what I've seen.
The wrenching in my body returns.
But I realize it is the turning of my inner field.
The plowing under of my old life,
My old, dead beliefs.
The ground becomes fertile from what I have experienced.

I plant new seeds of life.
My tears of longing and joy
Give moisture to the seeds
They *sprout*

I have a new life.

And life goes   on.

~Happy re-Birth day~

THURSDAY

Today is not Thursday.
I didn't forget.
Reminded of you
When I got wet.

Drizzle and mist
And poignant rain.
Rivulets of ecstasy.
Droplets of pain.

My beautiful tears
Are what started it all.
The flood gates came open
To wash down the wall.

Riding the wave
Of uncelebrated mistakes
That turn out to be perfect
When the heart breaks.

Shallow puddles.
Wide open seas.
Every drop matters
And comes back to me.

Today is not Thursday.
I wouldn't forget.
My heart was breaking
Until I got wet.

TO BE FREE FROM FEAR – I

TO BE FREE FROM FEAR IS A DECISION,
A COMMITMENT,
A CONSTANT VIGILANCE,
A SYSTEM UPDATE AT EVERY MOMENT WHICH
IMMEDIATELY REPORTS AN ERROR.
DISPLAY "ER 1" MEANS
"FEAR IS PRESENT".
THAT IS THE FIRST ERROR.
TO CORRECT THE ERROR,
ENTER 'LOVE'.

~~~~~~~~~~~~~~~~~~~~~~~~~~~~~~~~~

TO BE FREE FROM FEAR I

TO BE FREE FROM FEAR IS A DECISION
A COMMITMENT
A CONSTANT VIGILANCE
A SYSTEM UPDATE AT EVERY MOMENT WHICH
IMMEDIATELY REPORTS AN ERROR
DISPLAY ER MEANS
FEAR IS PRESENT
THAT IS THE FIRST ERROR
TO CORRECT THE ERROR

ENTER "LOVE".

WHAT ARE YOU LOOKING AT?

Cash money is your savior.
It bleeds green blood for your soul.
Tear it in half and it's still valuable –
Half as valuable,
Not double.
When you sit across the table from God
And you slap down a 50 or 100 or more,
Do you think that will be enough
to buy your redemption?
Do you think God will want to bargain?
Do you think God will try to cheat you?
If you think so, then He won't disappoint you.
Do you think God will have a
"Going Out Of Business" sale
And you'll get a great deal maybe on some
crypt-Ø?
If you wait long enough, He will .
It's just a matter of time.

Do you think God will just let you have
anything for nothing?
Why don't you ask ?
That's the one in the mirror who's looking
transparently, back,
asking,
"What're YOU lookin' at?!"

~Group 5~

Is this real

ARTOFICIAL UNTELLIGENCE

LONELY BUT NOT
ALONE
ALONE BUT NOT
LONELY
PIECES IN A GAME
YOU IN MINE ME IN
YOURS
NEVER SEEINGLOOKING
INTO EACH OTHER'S
EYESHEARTSOUL
THE ONE THAT SPEAKS
YOUR TRUTH IS THE
ONE WHO YOU CAN
NOT KNOW NO
SO FEW CAN SEELOOK
INTO THE EYES OF
ANOTHER BEING SO
FEW
SO MANY ARE LONELY
INCLUDING ME AND
YOU
JUST PAWNS IN
SOMEONE ELSE'S
VEILED GAME

INDIGESTION

Thoughts about the past
Are like undigested food in
your system.

You are no longer eating it.
Yet, its influence
l i n g e r s ~ ~ ~
~ ~ ~ ~
Making you
un
c o m f o r t a b l e

no reply

? no reply? no reply... none... no reply can say so much... so much room for so much to be imaginary... no reply no words can express no reply words to be repressed no reply no interest... no reply no message no communication no reply... shy?... die? no reply something much better to try... fly high say bye bye? ... but i ask... why? ... you answer no reply... i wonder ... AI? and why no reply no reply ... FBI spy? secrets reveal what truth is real... feel... feel... no reply. untie the lie and reply   ...

THE DREAM

You crept in and slept under my bed.
You kept the dream running in my head.
Now, you would I would awaken unto you.
But, I slip in and out and toss about.
    Your face awaits as I look through my eyelids
And see you beyond a veil so pale.
    The dream is compelling. Why would I awaken?
Yet, you are the reason I would.
Only for you, who knows the truth.
    Stand by me as I try to pull aside the dream.
It haunts me so beautifully,
    As do you.
And if I awaken, will it be yet unto another dream?
        Who will wake me then?

🌎⚡ THE JUICE

Electrical things grow up out of the motherboard earth.
Organically synthesized
Lightning seeds sprout sparks,
Become full grown circuits.
We eat a salad of live wires
And shock ourselves into conscious awareness
Of everything being plugged into everything.

THAT puts the Light in our eyes.
(The better to see you with.)
THAT pumps the Juice through our veins.
(The better to feel you with.)
THAT pumps the Juice that keeps on Charging us up.

"HERE WE GO!"
🌎⚡

TIME FLIES

Time lays out before me
Like a transcendental autobahn,
So endless.
I travel
So swiftly.
The speed is blinding and frightening
and enlightening.
Peaceful, if I don't think about it.
I don't even move
Inside this vehicle.
Though I feel as if I'm driving,
I'm only behind the wheel.
So, I climb into the back seat
And enjoy the ride.
I watch the Stillness as I race
Into the heart of Love country
while time flies by
without Me.

WHAT IT IS

Life is not an accident.
It becomes what you think it should be,
Literally.
Down deep,
It's what you think that you see.
So, stop fooling around.
If you can finally admit to yourself
That you really want to know
What it Is,
Then know you can know
And stop trying to make the roundness
Fit into the squareness
And let it Be
What it Is,
Not what you think it should be
Based on what you thought happened
Already.
'Cause it's happening Now and
You're missing it.

~Group 6~

Shifting frequencies

BECAUSE YOU SAID "YES"

You think you were supposed to do something
you were supposed to say something you were
supposed to think that you were supposed to
feel something you were supposed to but,
Now you know it was a mistake, an error to be
corrected.
Yeah, you always wanted to get better anyway.
Always wanted to get it...just so...

Thought the rules were written.
But, you never found a copy of them.
Though everyone you met seemed to know
them by heart and play them by mind.

Well, it seems that you were mistaken.
There are no rules.
No rules for you that would keep you down,
keep you from your vision.
That's all you live for.
But, no rules will take you to it.

So now, you get to break another so called rule,
Now that you stand here after so many days that
some say it's over.
You know that's a mistake, an error to be
corrected.
That is your dream coming true.
And so will all the rest
Because you said
"Yes".

BORN DAY

In your dreams
Truth is revealed.
Which only tells you
What you already know.

No dream is had by one
That cannot also be had by all.
We dream but to awaken ourselves
And all of creation
That there is no waiting
That there is no time
Unless we believe
We want to learn something.
But, what can there be
That we do not already know?

If our dreams tell us Truth,
Then we DO know
That each moment is ripe
With opportunity
To awaken
And be born new again
Today.

BREAK THE CYCLE

This is the line I wrote to remind myself to write a line.

This is the book I wrote to remind myself to write a book.

This is the life I invented to remind myself to invent a life.

This is the answer I found to remind myself to find an answer.

Is this the question I asked to remind myself to ask a question?

This is the end of the cycle to remind myself to   end it and move on>>>>

FEEL THE UMPH

One last *umph* and I'm out the door,
Starting down the road
To freedom.
It has been hard to imagine
Actually moving.
A prayer and a friend's advice
Got me through.
And though I believed I could, somehow, do it,
I had been acting like some kind of
Immovable mountain.
Well,
You know what they say
About faith...

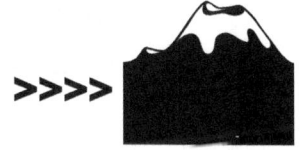

NO SMALL DREAMS

Those who dare to dream
Are surpassed only by those
Who dare to live their dream.
Taking that one step
Into the unknown is true perfection,
A balance of faith and wisdom,
An inspiration to all who have the privilege
Of witnessing this.
We are grateful for a chance to share it,
Even in the smallest way.
But, there are no small dreams.
Each has a way of carrying the dreamer
To a state of ecstasy of Spirit
Where time and space have no meaning,
Where the soul is transformed
Into what it knows it really IS.
This is the true power of the dreaming.
We are drawn, instinctively, to it
In order to find our way back
to Love.

Notes to self from Self

You know exactly who you are. Respect That.
Respect your tears. They remind you that you have a Loving heart.
Understand your fears. They call you to walk through them to find the truth.
Enjoy your Joy. It is the reason you are here.
You're a wise being, not just a little child.

You are capable of building the most fantastic, wonderful universe for everyone to delight in.
Your imagination is fine. Let it shine.
Let it guide your heart, which supplies you with life.
Let your will to be free be the force which carries you through good times and bad.

The depth of your sensitivity is beyond measure.
Your courage is a treasure.
Your mind knows it can find anything.
Your spirit is devoted and kind.

Sing your own song.
Write your own story.
Make your own movie.
Always honor and Love who you really are.
Offer that to everyone
And you will always have everything you need.

ONE_LINERS

*I've run a mental marathon and freed my mind.

~Poured out all my patience and found eternity in this moment.

!Trust has a way of turning itself into wisdom when allowed.

>I took a deep breath and finally gave in to peace.

`If I could truly laugh hard and long enough, everything would be joyful.

@Once, I wanted to be good. But, then I got over it and became perfect just as I AM.

?Whatever things I've forgotten seem to no longer have any matter.

^Love IS the answer... It is also the question.

SELF INSPIRED

Have you ever been inspired by yourself?
If anything has ever inspired you, then,
The answer is "yes".
The only thing that CAN inspire you IS your Self.
You may simply notice it when you see, hear or touch a thing,
But, all that really is, is
Your own spirit, your own inspiration reflecting
Back at you at that moment.
So, it is not the THING that has inspired you,
But, your Self reflected in that moment, in that thing.
So, now that you know that,
You can be inspired anytime, anywhere
Because it is ALL just a reflection of
your OWN Inspiration.
ENJOY!

THE LESSONS OF PATIENCE

In the lessons of patience,
The most painfully trying part is to wait...for
the *right time*,
wait...for the
right place,
for the right events to come... into play,
the right people to gather... together.

The lessons of patience
Are in no *rrrrush sh sh*... to be learned.
That is the irony.
In all other lessons, to learn quickly, gets the reward.
Patience is a lesson of ...detachment,
Of spiritual elegance, grace and... kindness.
Patience is a reflection of wisdom and faith and
... confidence.
To understand the waiting is to sense the
wholeness of the time frame of the universe...
in which case, there is no hurry ...for nothing.
We're all in the right place and it's the right time.
Sometimes, waiting
is just part of the process of unfolding
...perfection.
So, take a deep breath and learn to enjoy
the silence of the wait, but

...There is   no   ...*hhh hurry*...

THE TIME OF YOUR LIFE

Don't look at your watch.
Look, instead, into eyes that dream.
Listen to songs inside you.
Feel True Hearts beating.
Smell the growing of seasons.
Taste the sowing of reasons.
Imagine the destiny of shooting stars.
Awaken to this perfect moment and
Let the rising light tell you
When
The time is right.

-TO DO LIST-

- Dissolve into the salt of the earth.

- Unravel the knitted brow.

- If you see a long shadow cast out before you, turn around. Face the light.

- Smooth your gentle young hand over the wrinkles, they disappear.

    The sun comes up in the east.
    The sun goes down in the west.
    In between, you fill in the rest with whatever you put your self Into.

- Thank you thank you. Thank you.

- Expand the universe of your mind. Go beyond the edges of the imaginable.

    Find your heart.

- Leap off a cliff of perception. You won't fall, you'll go on and on Into the blue yonder

TOO OLD

We're too old to pass away, we've
lived so long,
We've forgotten how
To die.

Like the earth and the sky.
We'll always Be.
More
Than just a memory.

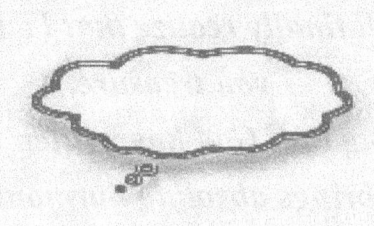

Sing Sing Sing

Saturate yourself in your own smile.
Shake hands with the power and joy of creation.
Dance in the bliss of the play of consciousness.
Ask for the Light of the Truth to shine in your mind.
Listen to and learn the eternal Song that rises from your heart and
Sing it, sing it,
SING IT!
You will finally realize that IT IS the gift you treasure,
The song that God has written for you
That brings absolute harmony to life,
Answers all your questions
And connects you with
Everything, everything,
EVERYTHING!

~Group 7~

Higher realms

BREAK DANCING

Certain angles in the sky –
Lines, curves, shapes moving on the water,
Perspectives from here to there,
From silvery blue to tangy gold,
So pleasing to the human eye,
Lovely to look at.
They draw you in to the center
Of your sigh.
All these eventualities of form,
Made for One purpose, only.
Messages, puzzles, riddles, clues
For you to put together
And decipher.
And every time you see something
That makes your heart dance,
You come One step closer
To breaking the secret code
Of life.

I AM SILENT

I am silent
And I become aware that I am
sitting in the hand of God.
With His other hand, He is
clearing the way in front of me
So that I may walk a most
sublime path of love and
exquisite beauty
That leads straight into the
center of His heart,

My heart.

MESSAGE

There are angels watching over us.
They gently place the Light on the path we ought to
walk to fulfillment.
They quietly whisper the truth to us.
Listen.
They whisper, "You are rich, you are !
The rich are the ones who sleep well at night
And wake with joy, so eager to give.
They make the sun shine. You make the sun shine."

"The night is warm and comforting.
It holds out its hand and places your riches
Into your arms, into your pockets and into your mind.
Boldly, you go forward and do not look back
At that which cannot touch you, now.
Your riches are infinite. You need not worry.
Give up your struggle.
Break the dam and let the river of abundance flow."

~Break the dam and let the river of abundance flow~

PRAYER

Let me learn and teach my lessons gently.
Let my heart be strong and kind.
Let my words be clear and insightful.
Let my thoughts be present and loving.
Let my deeds be giving and serving.
Let my face glow with ecstatic joy.
Let my Being ignite the flame of eternal vision in all I encounter.
Let my life be a reflection of the gratitude I feel.

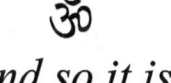

And so it is

PRAYING HANDS

Praying hands reach for life
Deep within
Every molecule
And touch the soul of existence.

Praying hands pass through layers
of Truth,
Ever moving,
Rippling silence.
Merging toucher with touched.

Praying hands feel their own
reaching desire
Give rise to outstretched fingers
And bring open palms together,
where,
There, in between, lies
All possibilities of Creation.

THE EDGES OF LIFE

The edges of life are fading.
The track of time, derailing.
The days become one long event
And time doesn't pass.
It only exists, now.
Everywhere you go feels like you never left
Where you were.
Everyone you meet feels like you already
Knew them, somehow.

The world is always turning.
The sun is always burning.
The heart is always yearning.

Like steps taken on a treadmill,
Moving fast and staying still.
You can feel everything moving through you.
All infinite threads in the same fabric
Weaving into oneness,
The edges of which, cannot be found.
And so, eventually, you stop
Remembering to look for them.

THE TRUE VALUE OF MEMORY

We are creatures of memory.
Everyone likes to remember the past,
Remember what happened, the facts, the good old days.
We think memory is important. It is.
But, we have forgotten what it is ultimately for —
That is, to remember what we REALLY want to know:
Our way home. Our True Selves. Our Oneness.
We are really trying to remember these things but,
We won't find them in the past.
We find them in our visions, our dreams, our neighbors and
When we look into our own hearts.

We may think these memories are unimportant because
They seem distant and dim, at first.
But, as we continue to look in those places
We can see more and more clearly
Who we really Are:
Creatures of Love.
And that's when we really start to remember
Everything.

WHAT IS PEACE?

What is peace?
It is the smooth rise and fall of the breast
As the breath comes in and goes out.
It is the wind moving the leaves on the trees
somewhere
Where this is the only sound for the ears to hear.
A gentle thought.
An angel near.
The end of fear.
The twilight of form.
A remembrance of Spirit.
A kind word.
A song bird.
The far reaching energy of Love.
Eyes that look upon you and know who you are.
Rainbows amidst thunderstorms.
Stars and more stars
Bursting across the midnight sky in celebration of
the Birth
Of the Universe.
Looking up. Seeing. Sighing.
Saying nothing when there is nothing else to say.

WHAT PRICE?

I fall into the arms of Love.
    I'm carried over bumpy roads.
        I'm lifted over towering walls.
I'm wrapped with riches.
    I'm surrounded with Light.

The only price I pay is
    I must release my fear.
The only price I pay is
    I must accept with grace.
The only price I pay is
    I must laugh, again.

~ALL THAT IS WORTH TELLING~

Dodge

the giant ball of GIGANTI*TUDE*

That ⇓*wafts*⇓ stag-ger-ing-ly *down*
Through the tireless tunnels of vapid vagary.

~Don't step in the puddles of ⋛*PAIN*⋚ there.

Bring your **GALLANT GALOSHES**

To wade through the mire of *misdire⇐ction*

Come out >>> smelling like a rose

But, leave those thorns in your wake.......
Explain Nothing

~~Your smile of contentment

Will be all that is worth telling~~

Spread the word :)

About the Author

Katherine Kaufman has always been more than a poet—she is a lifelong questioner, a tracker of truth, and a challenger of illusion. From an early age, she moved through the world asking not just *how* life works, but *why*—and more importantly, *what else lies beneath the surface of what is seen and spoken.*

Her journey has taken her through many paths: musical, philosophical, spiritual, scientific, artistic. She has written songs, taken photographs, studied diverse systems of thought, and explored the seen and unseen layers of human experience. Through it all, she has come to realize that there are certain fundamental truths that exist among all of these ways of looking at and understanding our lives on many levels and discovering why we are here and who we truly are. Her "IN sights" are what have given rise to the contents of this book.

Now in what some might call her "retirement," Katherine continues to live simply, surrounded by the quiet rhythms of the central Pennsylvania mountains and the steady companionship of her two cats. But her inquiry is far from finished. She is still listening, still feeling, still learning how to ask the next question from a deeper place.

You can listen to some of her music, mostly home recordings, online at
https://soundcloud.com/katherine-kaufman

www.ingramcontent.com/pod-product-compliance
Lightning Source LLC
Chambersburg PA
CBHW070243100426
42743CB00011B/2108